Anonymous

Rules and Regulations for the Government of the Woman's

Relief Corps

Anonymous

Rules and Regulations for the Government of the Woman's Relief Corps

ISBN/EAN: 9783337159139

Printed in Europe, USA, Canada, Australia, Japan

Cover: Foto ©ninafisch / pixelio.de

More available books at **www.hansebooks.com**

RULES AND REGULATIONS

FOR THE GOVERNMENT OF THE

Woman's Relief Corps,

AUXILIARY TO THE

GRAND ARMY OF THE REPUBLIC.

➤1894.◄

DECEMBER EDITION.

BOSTON :
E. B. STILLINGS & CO., PRINTERS,
55 SUDBURY STREET.

RULES AND REGULATIONS.

We, the mothers, wives, daughters and sisters of Union soldiers, sailors and marines who aided in putting down the Rebellion, do, with other loyal women, unite to establish a permanent association for the objects herein set forth, and through a National Convention do ordain and enact the following Rules and Regulations for its government.

CHAPTER I.

ARTICLE I.

NAME.

This Association shall be known as the Woman's Relief Corps, Auxiliary to the Grand Army of the Republic.

ARTICLE II.

OBJECTS.

SECTION 1. To specially aid and assist the Grand Army of the Republic and to perpetuate the memory of their heroic dead.

SECTION 2. To assist such Union veterans as need our help and protection, and to extend needful aid to their widows and orphans. To find them homes and employment, and assure them of sympathy and friends. To cherish and emulate the deeds of our army nurses, and of all loyal women who rendered loving service to our country in her hour of peril.

SECTION 3. To maintain true allegiance to the United States of America; to inculcate lessons of patriotism and love of country among our children and in the communities in which we live; and encourage the spread of universal liberty and equal rights to all.

ARTICLE III.

ORGANIZATION.

The several constituted bodies of this association shall consist of :

1. Subordinate organizations to be known as *. . . . . Relief Corps No. . . . . . Department of . . . . provided, however, that no Corps shall be organized except as auxiliary to a Post upon application approved and endorsed by the Post Commander. There can be but one Woman's Relief Corps auxiliary to the same Post.

2. State organizations to be known as Department of . . . . Woman's Relief Corps, Auxiliary to the Grand Army of the Republic.

* A Corps must bear the name of the Post to which it is auxiliary.

3. A National organization to be known as the National Convention of the Woman's Relief Corps, Auxiliary to the Grand Army of the Republic.

ARTICLE IV.

ELIGIBILITY TO MEMBERSHIP.

Women of good moral character and correct deportment, who have not given aid and comfort to the enemies of the Union, who would perpetuate the principles to which this association stands pledged, and who have attained the age of sixteen years, shall be eligible to membership in the Woman's Relief Corps.

CHAPTER II.

SUBORDINATE CORPS.

ARTICLE I.

FORMATION.

SECTION 1. A Corps may be formed by the authority of a Department President (or of the National President, where no Department organization exists), on the application of not less than ten persons eligible to membership in the Woman's Relief Corps; said application shall in all cases be accompanied by the charter fee of five dollars, and must be approved and endorsed by the Commander of the Post desiring an auxiliary Corps. There can be but one Woman's Relief Corps auxiliary to the same Post. The admission fee of charter members shall be the same as that of members admitted on application. No Corps shall be recognized by the members of the Woman's Relief Corps unless acting under a legal and unforfeited charter.

SECTION 2. On the receipt of such application, the Department President, (or National President where no Department organization exists), if satisfied of the eligibility of the applicants, and that it is for the interest of the Woman's Relief Corps to form such subordinate Corps, shall proceed, either in person or by detail, to organize the Corps, superintend the election of its officers for the remainder of the current year, and complete its organization. Only those obligated on the day the Corps is organized can become charter members, except should any have signed application for charter and were *unable* to be present at organization, they may, if initiated within a month, have their names enrolled on charter.

SECTION 3. Corps charters shall be signed by the Department President and countersigned by the Secretary of the Department within which the applicants for such charter reside.

SECTION 4. The rank of a Corps is established by the date of its charter. Date of organization shall appear upon charter and also upon Roster.

SECTION 5. A Corps charter may be surrendered voluntarily when less than ten members desire the continuance of the Corps. In case of surrender of a charter, the property of the Department, including Charter, Rituals, books of record and Corps papers, shall immediately be turned over to the Department Secretary and shall be subject to the disposition of the Department Council.

SECTION 6. A charter shall not be surrendered by any Corps so long as ten members thereof, in good standing, demand its continuance; nor unless a proposition to surrender the charter shall have been made at a regular meeting at least four weeks before the time of action, and written notice given to every member of the Corps; except, that upon official notification addressed to the Department President (or National President where no Department organization exists), that a Post desires the dissolution of its auxiliary, the charter shall be surrendered by the Corps upon command of the Department President (or National President), provided that the official notification of such desire shall not be considered, unless a majority of the members of the Post present and voting have voted in favor of such dissolution, after four weeks' previous notice.

SECTION 7. Corps charters may be suspended or annulled by the Department President (or National President where no Department organization exists), with the advice and consent of the Department Council.

SECTION 8. In case of revocation or surrender of a charter, all funds remaining in the treasury, after all indebtedness is paid, shall revert to the Post. Should the Post be disbanded or refuse to receive such funds, they shall revert to the Department for a Relief Fund, to be held for the purpose of relief only.

SECTION 9. A Corps having been disbanded or its charter annulled may be re-organized with its original name and number, provided these have not been appropriated. In such re-organization a new charter shall be issued, according to the provisions of Sections 1 and 2 of this Article.

ARTICLE II.

ADMISSION TO MEMBERSHIP.

SECTION 1. Every application for admission to membership shall be made on the regularly prepared blanks issued from National Headquarters, be signed by the applicant, with full personal name, and must be accompanied by an admission fee of not less than one dollar, and price of badge added thereto. Members leaving the Order must return their badges, for which the regular price will be paid.

SECTION 2. The application shall be recommended by two members of the Corps, who vouch for the applicant's eligibility by their signatures — be presented at a regular meeting, and referred to a committee of three, whose duty it is to investigate and report.

Neither member recommending applicant shall act on investigating committee.

SECTION 3. After careful investigation, the committee will, by their signature, approve or disapprove the application, and report at a subsequent regular meeting of the Corps; *provided*, however, that in special cases only the National President or Department President may grant a dispensation in writing to a Corps permitting an investigating Committee to report on the day of their appointment. An application may be withdrawn while in the hands of an investigating committee; but be the report favorable or unfavorable, *after committee has reported* it must take its regular course, except it should, upon discussion, appear that the committee reported without proper investigation. The Corps may then decline to vote, the committee be discharged, and a new one appointed. Should a member of the committee be absent or decline to report, the President may declare a vacancy and fill the same.

SECTION 4. After the application is read and committee report, the President shall give opportunity to any member having objections to the applicant's election to state the same, after which a ballot with ball ballots shall be had. If, on counting the ballots deposited, it appears that twenty or less were cast, and four or more of them are black, the candidate is rejected; should the result of the ballot be unfavorable to the applicant, the President may, *before declaring the vote*, order a second ballot, the result of which shall be final. If *more* than twenty are cast, then an additional black ball for every additional ten, or fractional part thereof, shall be necessary to reject. If *less* than four black balls be cast, the candidate shall be declared elected. No reconsideration of a ballot shall be had after the President has announced the result thereof.

SECTION 5. Each applicant, upon her election, shall be at once notified in writing, and on presenting herself for membership, shall be properly initiated. But unless she present herself for initiation within three months from the date of such notice, her election shall be void, and all moneys which accompanied the application shall be forfeited to the Corps treasury.

SECTION 6. If an applicant be rejected, she shall be at once notified of the fact in writing, and the admission fee shall be returned. She shall not be eligible to admission to the Woman's Relief Corps for six months after such rejection. A second, and all subsequent applications, shall be in the same form, and subject to the same conditions as the first.

SECTION 7. An applicant having been regularly elected, may be initiated at a special meeting.

A Department President may, in any special case, authorize a Corps by written dispensation to initiate a candidate who has not presented herself for initiation within three months after notice of election, such request to be by two-thirds vote of the Corps.

Should an applicant after being elected prove to be unworthy, the Corps may by a two-thirds vote petition the Department President to set aside the ballot and annul the election.

SECTION 8. The Department President may, within her jurisdiction, and at her discretion, receive and initiate an applicant for membership, or detail a member for that purpose, provided such applicant reside outside the proper territorial limits of any Corps. A member thus received shall be granted a transfer card signed by the Department President and Secretary bearing the same date as initiation.

SECTION 9. Where no Department organization exists, the National President shall have the same jurisdiction as a Department President.

SECTION 10. A member-elect, upon initiation, shall subscribe to these Rules and Regulations and the By-Laws of the Corps; and receive from the Corps a membership badge, which shall be worn upon the left breast, at all meetings of the Woman's Relief Corps.

ARTICLE III.
ADMISSION OF MEMBERS BY TRANSFER.

SECTION 1. A member having a valid transfer card may, upon regular application, and presenting herself for admission by transfer, be re-admitted to the Corps which granted the same after her name has been proposed, referred and reported upon, and upon receiving a two-thirds vote by ballot of the members present and voting at a regular meeting; or she may be admitted to another Corps, upon regular application as above, and presenting herself for admission by transfer, by a two-thirds vote by ballot of the members present and voting at a regular meeting; or she may be admitted a charter member of a new Corps.

SECTION 2. Each Corps may, through its By-Laws, establish such an admission fee as they think proper to be paid by members joining by transfer, the amount not to exceed that paid at a regular initiation.

ARTICLE IV.
VISITING, TRANSFER AND DISCHARGE CARDS.

SECTION 1. Any member applying therefor in person or by letter shall be granted a visiting card signed by the President, and attested by the Secretary, for a specified time not exceeding twelve months, commending her to all members, provided she has faithfully discharged all duties enjoined upon her and has paid in advance all dues for the time specified in the visiting card.

SECTION 2. Any member against whom no charges exist and who has paid all dues, shall receive a transfer card signed by the President and attested by the Secretary, upon verbal or written application to the President at a regular meeting of the Corps. Upon its presentation to any Corps, within one year from date of issue, she may be admitted in the manner prescribed in Art. III of this chapter. In the meantime she shall remain, for purposes of discipline only, under the jurisdiction of the Corps granting the transfer card. A member holding transfer card is not entitled to the password. If at the expiration of a year she has not been admitted to membership in any Corps, and no charges have been preferred, the transfer card shall be void, and the holder be considered honorably discharged from the Order.

SECTION 3. Members of disbanded Corps who were in good standing at the time of such dissolution shall receive transfer cards from the Department Secretary which shall have full force.

SECTION 4. Department Presidents may grant a special dispensation to a member out on transfer (but not within reach of another

Corps) permitting her to be considered a member of the Corps from which the transfer was taken until such time as she shall be able to present herself to some Corps for admission by transfer, as prescribed in the Ritual.

SECTION 5.   Any member in good standing, on written application to the Corps President at a regular meeting, shall receive at some subsequent meeting, on the return of her badge, an honorable discharge signed by the President and attested by the Secretary.   A member thus discharged can be re-admitted by filing a new application to be regularly referred and reported upon, and upon receiving a two-thirds vote by ballot of the members present and voting at a regular meeting, she shall be admitted without re-initiation on taking anew the obligation.

SECTION 6.   A member can be dishonorably discharged only upon due trial and sentence as per Chap. V, Art. VII.

ARTICLE V.

MEETINGS.

SECTION 1.   The regular meetings of each Corps shall be held at least monthly.

SECTION 2.   Special meetings may be called by the Corps President, or upon the written request of five members of the Corps. Notice thereof must be given to each member of the Corps, and the object of such meeting stated, and no business shall be transacted except such as is specified in the call.

SECTION 3.   Eight members qualified to transact business shall constitute a quorum at any meeting of the Corps.

SECTION 4.   Corps having thirty or less members, *five* members qualified to transact business *may* constitute a quorum; the chairs to be filled being President, Secretary, Treasurer, Conductor and Guard.

SECTION 5.   Children over two years of age cannot be admitted to Corps meetings.

ARTICLE VI.

OFFICERS.

SECTION 1.   All members of the Woman's Relief Corps in good standing are eligible to any Corps, Department or National office.

SECTION 2.   The officers of each Corps shall be a President, Senior and Junior Vice-Presidents, Secretary, Treasurer, Chaplain, Conductor, Guard, Assistant Conductor and Assistant Guard.

SECTION 3.   The Corps President shall appoint Relief. Executive, Auditing, Home and Employment and Conference Committees, to be directors of Corps work.

SECTION 4.   The terms of appointed officers and committees (Corps, Department or National) expire with the appointing power.   They shall hold office until their successors are appointed, but may at any time be removed at the option of the appointing officer.

ARTICLE VII.

ELECTION OF OFFICERS.

SECTION 1.   The Corps officers, except Secretary, Assistant Conductor and Assistant Guard, shall be elected at the first regular meeting in December, or at a special meeting if necessary to conclude the election. Each member of the Corps in good standing must be previously notified. The election shall be by written ballot, unless such ballot be dispensed with by unanimous consent.

SECTION 2. In balloting for officers, a majority of all the votes cast shall be necessary to a choice. If there is no election on the first two ballots, the name of the member receiving the lowest number of votes shall be dropped, and so on in successive ballots until a choice is made.

SECTION 3. The officers thus elected shall be installed at the first regular meeting in January following, or at a special meeting called for such purpose during the month (except officers of Corps organized in December, who being then installed hold office for the year). The newly elected officers shall select the Installing Officer, the Corps Secretary immediately reporting their choice to the Department Secretary. If a member from another Corps be selected, the appointment will be made by the Department President, upon the request of officers elect. At the installation the Corps President shall appoint the Secretary; the Conductor and Guard respectively nominate the Assistant Conductor and Assistant Guard, who, when confirmed by the President, shall also be installed. All officers enter upon their duties immediately after installation, and, whether elected or appointed, hold office until their successors are installed. Installation may be conducted publicly.

SECTION 4. At the first regular meeting after the installation of officers, the President shall appoint the Committees as provided for in Chap. II, Article VI, Section 3.

SECTION 5. Corps may fill any vacancy in their elective offices at any regular meeting, provided notice of such contemplated action has been given at a previous meeting.

ARTICLE VIII.
DUTIES OF OFFICERS.

SECTION 1. It is the duty of a Corps President to preside at all meetings of the Corps, to enforce a strict observance of the Rules and Regulations of the Order and By-Laws of the Corps, and all orders from proper authority; to detail all officers and committees not otherwise provided for; to approve by her signature all orders drawn by the Secretary upon the Treasurer for appropriations of money made and passed at a regular meeting of the Corps; to forward the reports and returns required by Rules and Regulations, and perform such other duties as may appertain to her office. She shall forward to the Post Commander a quarterly report of the relief extended by the Corps, and confer with him concerning all matters in common between Post and Corps. She shall appoint a Conference Committee of five to meet and counsel with a like Committee from the Post, in order to strengthen the relations and perfect the work for which these organizations are mutually pledged. She shall signify to the Post Commander her desire for the appointment of such Committee.

SECTION 2. The Vice-Presidents shall perform such duties as are required of them by the Ritual, and in the absence of the President shall fill her office according to seniority. If neither of them are present the next regular officer in rank calls meeting to order, when the Corps shall elect a President pro tem.

SECTION 3. The Secretary shall keep in books properly prepared:

1. The Rules and Regulations of the Woman's Relief Corps and the By-Laws of the Corps, to be duly signed by every member upon initiation.

2. A Journal, in which must be recorded the minutes of each meeting of the Corps and from which the same shall be read to the Corps at a regular meeting. Her signature, or that of the Secretary pro tem., must attest all proceedings after being corrected and approved.

3. An Order Book, in which shall be recorded all orders drawn on the Treasurer, and approved by the President.

4. A General Order File, in which shall be preserved all orders and circulars issued by Department or National Headquarters, in the order in which they are received.

5. A Letter File, in which shall be preserved all official correspondence.

6. The Secretary shall draw all orders for money on the Treasurer, approved by the Corps President; shall in writing notify all applicants for membership the result of ballot, and, under the direction of the President, prepare all reports and returns required of her ; she shall notify the Department Secretary of the death of any army nurse that may be known to her ; and shall perform such other duties as appertain to her office, and transfer to her successor, without delay, all books, papers and other Corps property in her possession.

SECTION 4. The Treasurer shall hold the funds, vouchers and other property of the Corps, pay all orders for money drawn by the Secretary and approved by the Corps President, and collect all moneys due the Corps, giving her receipt therefor; disburse no moneys except upon regularly drawn orders ; keep an account with each member, *notify in writing all members in arrears,* and furnish the President with a list of the same, and render to the Corps at each regular meeting in writing an account of its finances, which shall be referred to the Finance Committee. She shall make and deliver to the President all reports required of Corps Treasurers, by Chap. V, Art. I, and deliver to her successor in office, or to any one designated by the Corps, all moneys, books and other property of the Corps in her possession or under her control. She shall give bonds prior to her installation, in a sum to be named by the Corps, for the faithful discharge of her duties.

SECTION 5. The Chaplain shall officiate at the opening of the Corps and at the funeral of members when attended by the Corps. She shall compile the records of Memorial Day and promptly forward the same to Department Chaplain through Corps President, not later than June 10, and perform such other duties in connection with her office as the Corps may require.

SECTION 6. The Conductor and Guard shall perform such duties as may be required by the Ritual or the Corps President.

SECTION 7. The Assistant Conductor and Assistant Guard shall assist the Conductor and the Guard respectively, in their duties.

SECTION 8. The several Committees shall have the control of such property as the Corps by vote shall place in their possession, subject to the direction of the Corps as to its management and investment.

SECTION 9. The Relief Committee shall have the management of the Relief Fund, subject to the direction of the Corps. They shall investigate all applications for relief, supply temporal wants, visit the sick, bury the dead, and report to the Corps monthly, in writing, all duties performed. All bills contracted by the Committee shall be audited by the chairman before presentation to the Corps for action.

SECTION 10. The Executive Committee shall devise methods for obtaining funds, and aid in carrying into execution all such methods as are approved by the Corps. This Committee shall be prepared for special calls, arrange for Memorial Day, and present a written report to the Corps of all duties performed. All bills contracted by the Committee shall be audited by the chairman, before presentation to the Corps for action.

SECTION 11. The Auditing Committee shall examine the books and accounts of the Treasurer and other officers quarterly, report in writing, and perform such other duties as may be required of them by the Corps. A single member of the Committee has not the right to audit the books; a majority is necessary.

SECTION 12. The Home and Employment Committee shall secure the admission of veterans' orphans to homes provided for them by city or state, or in private families; find employment for those who are in need, and secure the admission of the sick and friendless widows, army nurses and orphans to hospitals or other places of refuge. The Chairman shall present a written report to the Corps monthly.

SECTION 13. The Conference Committee shall meet a like Committee from the Post, to confer concerning matters of mutual interest, in order to strengthen the relations and perfect the work for which these organizations are mutually pledged.

SECTION 14. The Corps Treasurer shall turn over to committees such property and funds as the Corps by vote may direct. Such additional committees may be provided as Corps work may demand.

ARTICLE IX.

DELEGATES.

Each Corps shall, at the first regular meeting in December, annually elect, from its members in good standing, delegates, and an equal number of alternates to the Department Convention, in the manner prescribed in Chap. III, Art. II.

ARTICLE X.

BY-LAWS.

Corps may adopt By-Laws for their government, not inconsistent with these Rules and Regulations, the Service Book, or Orders of the Department or National Conventions, and may provide for the alteration or amendment thereof.

Corps By-Laws must be submitted to Department Presidents for approval or correction before being adopted.

CHAPTER III.

DEPARTMENTS.

ARTICLE I.

ORGANIZATION.

SECTION 1. A Department may be formed (where no Department organization exists) upon the application of not less than five subordinate Corps of the Woman's Relief Corps, auxiliary to the Grand Army of the Republic, such application to be accompanied in all cases by a charter fee of ten dollars.

SECTION 2. On receipt of such application the National President shall, if satisfied that it is for the interest of the Woman's Relief Corps to form such Department, proceed, either in person or by detail, to organize the Department, superintend the election of its officers for the remainder of the current year and complete its organization.

SECTION 3. Department Charters shall be signed by the National President, countersigned by the National Secretary, and shall bear date of organization.

SECTION 4. Each Department shall be governed by a Department Convention, subordinate to the National Convention.

SECTION 5. The National Convention at its annual session, or the National President, with the consent of the National Council, may at any time revoke the charter of a Department which has failed to forward its reports for three successive quarters; or for general incompetency it may be remanded to a Provisional Department by the same authority.

ARTICLE II.

MEMBERSHIP.

SECTION 1. The Department Convention shall consist of : —

1. The National President, Past National Presidents, Past National Vice-Presidents, Past National Secretaries, and Past National Treasurers, in their respective Departments, so long as they remain in good standing in their respective Corps.

2. The Department President and all Past Department Presidents who have served a full term, or who, having been elected to fill a vacancy, shall have served to the end of the term, and Past Department Secretaries and Past Department Treasurers, so long as they remain in good standing in their respective Corps; and the other officers mentioned in Art. IV, Sect. 2, of this Chapter.

3. All Corps Presidents throughout the Department,—in the absence of the Corps President the Vice-President, according to seniority, may represent the Corps. All Past Corps Presidents who have served a full term (except in Departments which have otherwise provided by a two-thirds vote at an annual meeting), or who, having been elected to fill a vacancy, shall have served to the end of the term, so long as they remain in good standing in their respective Corps.

4. Delegates regularly elected by the several Corps in such ratio as may have been determined by the previous Annual Convention, and one additional delegate for a final fraction of more than one-half of that number.

SECTION 2. The number of delegates to which each Corps is entitled shall be determined by the quarterly report of September 30 preceding, each Corps being entitled to one delegate, whatever its membership.

SECTION 3. Corps organized after September 30 and prior to January 1 will elect delegates in the same ratio as above.

SECTION 4. Corps organized on and after January 1 will be represented by their President only (or Vice-President, according to seniority).

SECTION 5. These delegates, and an equal number of alternates, shall be chosen at the same time and in the same manner of electing Corps officers at the first regular meeting in December, and shall serve during the year, commencing on the first day of January following. Any vacancies that occur may be filled as provided in Chap. II, Art. VII, Sect. 5, and notice of such election must be immediately forwarded to the Department Secretary.

SECTION 6. The Installing Officer shall immediately after Installation forward to the Department Secretary a list of newly elected officers, delegates and alternates, as provided in Chap. V, Art. II, Sect. 1.

ARTICLE III.
MEETINGS.

SECTION 1. There shall be an annual meeting of each Department Convention, at the same time and in the same town or city where the Department Encampment of the Grand Army of the Republic is held; provided, that if accommodations are inadequate for both, Convention shall be held at some contiguous point. A semi-annual meeting may be held, if so determined at the annual meeting of the Department or by the Department Council.

SECTION 2. Special meetings of the Department Convention may be called by the Department President, by and with the advice and consent of the Department Council, and no business shall be transacted except that specified in the call. No alterations affecting the general interests of the Department shall be made at a special meeting.

ARTICLE IV.
OFFICERS.

SECTION 1. All members of the Woman's Relief Corps in good standing are eligible to any Corps, Department or National office.

SECTION 2. The officers of each Department are a President, Senior Vice-President, Junior Vice-President, Secretary, Treasurer, Chaplain, Inspector, Counselor, Instituting and Installing Officer, and an Executive Board of five members. These officers constitute the Department Council.   The five members are elected by the Department Convention as the Executive Board for the year, and the first elected shall be chairman.

ARTICLE V.
ELECTION OF OFFICERS.

SECTION 1.   The Department officers (except the Secretary, Inspector, Counselor and Instituting and Installing Officer, who are appointed by the Department President) shall be elected annually at the Department Convention by written ballot, unless such ballot be dispensed with by unanimous consent.

SECTION 2.   These officers shall enter upon their respective duties immediately after their installation, and hold office until their successors are installed.

SECTION 3.   Vacancies occurring in Department elective offices, either by death, written resignation or otherwise, shall be filled by the Department Council, duly called and sitting within its own jurisdiction, or by written acquiescence in the recommendation of the Department President by two-thirds of the Council.

ARTICLE VI.
DUTIES OF OFFICERS.

SECTION 1.   The Department President, immediately upon assuming the duties of her office, shall appoint a Department Secretary, Inspector, Counselor, and Instituting and Installing Officer. She shall, upon the nomination of the Department Inspector, appoint as many Assistant Inspectors as may be required; also all Department officers and committees not otherwise provided for, and as many Aides as she may deem necessary.

She shall enforce the Rules and Regulations of the Woman's Relief Corps and all orders from proper authority; for this purpose she may issue such orders as may be necessary.   She shall preside in Department Convention and Department Council, approve all orders for money properly drawn on the Department Treasurer, and hold as trustee for the Department all securities given by Department officers; promulgate through the proper channels a Department password, and change the same at her discretion; she shall present to Department Encampment, through Department Commander, a brief report of relief work done by her Department during the year; sign and forward all reports due National Headquarters, also the per capita tax; issue charters to all Corps regularly organized in her Department; attest, by her signature, the reports of Department Chaplain, Inspector, and Instituting and Installing Officer, forward them to the respective National Officers, and perform such other duties as are incumbent upon the office.

SECTION 2.   The Department Vice-Presidents shall assist the President, by counsel or otherwise, and in her absence or disability shall fill her office according to seniority.

SECTION 3.   The Department Secretary shall conduct the official correspondence and issue all orders under the direction of the Department President; keep correct records of the proceedings of Department Convention and Department Council, and prepare the minutes of the Convention and reports of officers for publication, if so ordered by the Convention; draw all orders for money upon the Department Treasurer approved by the Department President; prepare all reports and returns to National Headquarters and transmit the same, through the Department President, to the National Secretary; and with the last quarterly report, before retiring from office, a detailed report of the condition of Corps and membership, for filing with the National Secretary; she shall forward to Corps Presidents, each quarter, Corps Secretary's Blanks, Form A, Corps Treasurer's Blanks Form B, Corps Relief Reports Form N, and with first quarter's report blanks Memorial Day Blanks Form J, and at least ten days prior to Corps Elections Corps Election Returns Form L; shall forward to Corps Installing Officers Consolidated Report Corps Installation Form U, and Assistant Instituting and Installing Officer Blank Form G to the officer designated to institute a Corps in her Department; notify the Secretary of the Home Board of the death of any Army Nurse that may be known to her; forward name and residence of Department Chaplain to National Chaplain immediately after Department Conventions; forward all General Orders to outgoing, incoming and permanent representatives of National Convention; countersign all charters issued by the President; keep an Order Book, a General Order File, and Letter File; file all orders, reports and official correspondence; furnish list of all persons in the Department entitled to receive a copy of Journal of Proceedings of National Convention; and perform such other duties and keep such other records in connection with her office as may be required of her by the Department President or the Department Convention, and receive as compensation for her services such sum as the Department Convention may determine.

SECTION 4. The Department Treasurer shall hold the funds, vouchers and other property of the Department, fill all orders for supplies made on regular requisition blanks, receive all moneys due the Department, giving her receipt therefor, pay all orders properly drawn by the Department Secretary and approved by the Department President, and disburse no moneys except upon regularly drawn orders. She shall forward through Department President all reports and dues required by Rules and Regulations, furnish to Corps a quarterly statement of their indebtedness, and a duplicate statement to the Department President, and upon retiring from office furnish her successor a list of supplies on hand, also one of such supplies as will be needed at once, and give a bond in a sum to be fixed by the Department Convention, with sufficient sureties, to be approved by the Department President, for the faithful discharge of her duties, and receive as compensation for her services such sum as the Department Convention may determine.

SECTION 5. The Department Chaplain shall compile the Memorial Day reports forwarded by Corps Chaplains, and make consolidated report for the information of the Department President, sign and transmit a copy of each to the National Chaplain through the Department President, not later than June 20, and perform such other duties in connection with her office as the Department President or the Department Convention may require of her.

SECTION 6. The Department Inspector shall perform such duties as are prescribed in Chap. V, Art. V, under direction of the Department President.

SECTION 7. The Department Counselor shall familiarize herself with the Rules and Regulations, the official decisions of the Woman's Relief Corps, and be prepared to aid the Department President and Department Council, when called upon to do so, and perform such other duties as may be required of her by the Department President.

SECTION 8. . The Department Instituting and Installing Officer shall fit herself to properly organize and instruct Corps and install officers, when so directed by the Department President. She shall make a quarterly report on Form H, for the information of the Department President, sign and affix her post-office address and transmit a copy of the same to National Instituting and Installing Officer through the Department President, at the same time reports are due at National Headquarters, and perform such other duties as may be assigned her.

SECTION 9. The Department Council shall meet prior to, and immediately following, the Department Convention, and at such other times and places as the Department President may order, or at the written request of five members; and five members shall constitute a quorum. They shall keep a full and detailed record of their proceedings and submit the same through the Department Secretary as their report to the Department Convention for their consideration. Unless legalized by that body they have no force or standing in law.

SECTION 10. The Executive Board shall hold its meetings at such time and place as the Department President may order, or at the written request of three members, and shall counsel with the Department President in matters affecting the welfare of the Department, and report to the Department Council at the meeting held prior to the opening of Department Convention. They shall select from their number an Auditing Committee, who shall audit the accounts of the Treasurer quarterly, and report at such times as the Board may direct.

SECTION 11. The several Staff Officers shall make to the Department Convention — through the Department Secretary — full and complete reports, in writing, of the official duties performed in their respective Departments, and when retiring from office shall deliver to their successors all moneys, books or other property of the Department in their possession or under their control.

ARTICLE VII.
VOTING.

Each representative present at a meeting of the Department Convention shall be entitled to one vote. Members entitled to representation by virtue of past office, shall be entitled to but *one* vote. The ayes and noes may be required and entered upon record at the call of any three members representing different Corps.

ARTICLE VIII.
DELEGATES.

Delegates to the National Convention shall be chosen as provided in Art. 11 of this Chapter.

ARTICLE IX.

BY-LAWS.

Department Conventions may adopt By-Laws for the government of the Department not inconsistent with these Rules and Regulations, the Service Book, or Orders of the National Convention, and may provide for the alteration and amendment thereof.

CHAPTER IV.

ARTICLE I.

NATIONAL CONVENTION.

The supreme power of the Woman's Relief Corps is the National Convention.

ARTICLE II.

MEMBERSHIP.

SECTION 1. The National Convention shall consist of:—

1. The National President, Past National Presidents and Past National Vice-Presidents, Past National Secretaries and Past National Treasurers, so long as they remain in good standing in their respective Corps, and the other officers named in Art. IV, Sect. 2, of this Chapter.

2. Of the Presidents, Vice-Presidents, Secretaries and Treasurers of the several Departments.

3. Of the Presidents and Secretaries of Provisional Departments, and Presidents of all Detached Corps where no Department organization exists.

4. Of Past Department Presidents who have served a full term, or who having been elected to fill a vacancy shall have served to the end of the term, so long as they remain in good standing in their several Corps.

5. Of one delegate at large from each Department, and one delegate for each seven hundred members, and one additional delegate for a final fraction of more than one-half of that number, in good standing at the close of the fourth quarter ending December 31; such delegates to be elected by the Department Convention, at the same time and in the same manner of electing Department officers. Departments having less than seven hundred members shall be entitled to but one delegate—a delegate at large. Each Department shall be entitled to one delegate whatever its membership.

SECTION 2. Each Department shall also elect, at the same time and in the same manner, an equal number of alternates, including an alternate at large. Only the above officers, and delegates or their alternates, shall be admitted to seats, except as provided in Chap. III, Art. V, Sec. 3.

SECTION 3. The Installing Officer shall, immediately after installation, forward to the National Secretary a list of the newly elected officers, delegates and alternates, as provided in Chap. V, Art. II, Sec. 2, and transmit a copy of the same to the National Secretary for the information of the National President.

ARTICLE III.
MEETINGS.

SECTION 1. The National Convention shall be held annually at the same time, and in the town or city where the National Encampment of the Grand Army of the Republic is held; provided, that if accommodations are inadequate for both, Convention shall be held at some contiguous point.

SECTION 2. Special meetings of the National Convention may be called by the National President, by and with the advice and consent of the National Council, and no business shall be transacted except that specified in the call. No alterations affecting the general interests of the Order shall be made at a special meeting.

ARTICLE IV.
OFFICERS.

SECTION 1. All members of the Woman's Relief Corps in good standing are eligible to any Corps, Department or National office.

SECTION 2. The National officers of the Woman's Relief Corps are a National President, National Senior and Junior Vice-Presidents, National Secretary, National Treasurer, National Chaplain, National Inspector, National Counselor, National Instituting and Installing Officer and a National Executive Board. These officers constitute the National Council. The five members elected by National Convention annually, and the life members, constitute the Executive Board for the year, of which the first elected shall be chairman.

SECTION 3. The five elected members of the National Woman's Relief Corps Home Board shall be recognized as National officers during their term of office and be voting members of National Convention. They shall be obligated the same as all other National officers.

ARTICLE V.
ELECTION OF OFFICERS.

SECTION 1. The National Officers of the Woman's Relief Corps (except the National Secretary, National Inspector, National Counselor, and National Instituting and Installing Officer, who are appointed by the President), shall be elected annually at the National Convention by written ballot unless such ballot be dispensed with by unanimous consent.

SECTION 2. These officers shall enter upon their respective duties immediately after their installation, and hold office until their successors are installed.

SECTION 3. Vacancies occurring in National elective offices shall be filled by the National Council, either at a special meeting or by written acquiescence in the recommendation of the National President by two-thirds of the Council.

ARTICLE VI.

DUTIES OF OFFICERS.

SECTION 1. The National President, immediately upon assuming the duties of her office, shall appoint a National Secretary, National Inspector, National Counselor, and National Instituting and Installing Officer, and as many Assistant National Inspectors and Aides as she may deem necessary. She shall appoint all other National officers and committees not otherwise provided for.

She shall enforce the Rules and Regulations of the Woman's Relief Corps, and the orders of the National Convention and National Council, and for this purpose she may issue such orders as may be necessary. She shall preside in National Convention and National Council, and decide all questions of law or usage, subject to an appeal to the National Convention; approve all orders for money properly drawn on the National Treasurer, and hold as trustee for the Woman's Relief Corps all securities given by National officers. She shall promulgate through the proper officers the National password and may change the same at her discretion; shall issue charters to all Departments when regularly organized, and may appoint Provisional Presidents where no Department organization exists.

SECTION 2. The National Vice-Presidents shall assist the National President by counsel or otherwise, and in her absence or disability, shall fill her office according to seniority.

SECTION 3. The National Secretary shall conduct the official correspondence and issue all orders, under direction of the National President; keep correct records of the proceedings of the National Convention and Council, and prepare the minutes of the Convention and reports of officers for publication if so ordered by the Convention. All reports received by her from Departments shall be turned over to the proper officers. She shall prepare all blanks and books required for the use of the Woman's Relief Corps. She shall forward to Department Presidents, each quarter, Department Secretary's Blank Form C, Department Treasurer's Blank Form D, Department Secretary's Consolidated Blank Form E, Department Treasurer's Consolidated Blank Form F, and at least thirty days prior to Department Convention, Department Election Returns Form M, and Department Treasurer's Bonds; and Department Delinquent Blanks Form V., with the report blanks for quarter ending June 30 each year. She shall forward to Detached Corps Presidents, each quarter, Corps Secretary's Blank Form A, Corps Treasurer's Blank Form B, Corps Relief Reports Form N; and at least ten days prior to Corps Elections, Corps Election Returns Form L, and Corps Treasurer's Bond. She shall forward Assistant Instituting and Installing Officer's Blank Form G to the officer designated to institute a Detached Corps; shall draw all orders for money on the National Treasurer, approved by the National President, and perform such other duties and keep such books and records as may be required of her by the National President or National Convention. She shall forward to National Chaplain a correct list of names and addresses of Department Chaplains and Presidents of Detached Corps. She shall prepare a list of suspended Detached Corps for the information of her successor and give a bond in the sum of one thousand dollars or such amount as shall be voted by the National Convention, with sufficient sureties to be approved by the National President, and receive such compensation for her services as the National Convention may determine.

SECTION 4. The National Treasurer shall hold all funds and vouchers of the National Convention, order all supplies under direction of the National President, receive all moneys due the National Convention, giving her receipt therefor, pay all orders drawn on her by the National Secretary, and approved by the National President, disburse no moneys except upon regularly drawn orders, fill all orders for supplies for the use of the Woman's Relief Corps, made by Department Treasusers on regular requisition blanks, and under the direction of the National President charge a reasonable and uniform price for the same. She shall furnish to Departments and Detached Corps quarterly statements of their indebtedness and a duplicate statement to the National President, and give a bond in the sum of five thousand dollars, or such amount as shall be voted by National Convention, with sufficient sureties to be approved by the National President, for the faithful discharge of her duties, and receive such compensation for her services as the National Convention may determine.

SECTION 5. The National Chaplain shall consolidate the Memorial Day reports of Department Chaplains, and, in her annual report, make such recommendations as will advance the charitable and fraternal work of the Order, and perform such duties in connection with her office as the National President or National Convention may require. She shall forward Department Chaplain's Report blanks Form K to Department Chaplains, and Memorial Day blanks Form J to Detached Corps.

SECTION 6. The National Inspector shall perform such duties as are required in Chap. V, Art. V, under direction of the National President.

SECTION 7. The National Counselor shall familiarize herself with the Rules and Regulations and the official decisions of the Woman's Relief Corps, and be prepared to aid the National President and National Council, when called upon to do so, and perform such other duties as may be required of her by the National President.

SECTION 8. The National Instituting and Installing Officer shall forward Department Instituting and Installing Officers' blanks Form H to Department Instituting and Installing Officers; shall receive and consolidate the reports of Department Instituting and Installing Officers on Form I, also National Aides, and the organization of Provisional Departments, compiling the same for the information of the National President, sign and transmit a copy of the same to the National Secretary, and perform such other duties as may be assigned her.

SECTION 9. The National Council shall meet prior to and immediately following the National Convention, and at such other times and places as the National President may order, or at the written request of five members; and five members shall constitute a quorum. They shall keep full and detailed records of their proceedings, and present the same as their report to the National Convention, for the consideration of that body.

SECTION 10. The Executive Board shall hold its meetings at such time and place as the National President may order, or at the written request of three members, and shall counsel with the National President in matters affecting the welfare of the National Association, and report to the National Council at the meeting held prior to the opening of National Convention. They shall select from their number an Auditing Committee, who shall audit the accounts of the Treasurer annually, and report at such times as the Board may direct.

SECTION 11. The National Woman's Relief Corps Home Board shall hold its meetings at such time and place as the laws governing the Home provide. They shall have charge of the working interests of the Home, and make regular statements to the National President and annual reports to National Convention.

SECTION 12. The several Staff Officers shall present to the National Convention, through the National Secretary, full and detailed reports in print of the official duties performed in their respective Departments, and when retiring from office shall deliver to their successors all moneys, books or other property of the Woman's Relief Corps in their possession or under their control.

ARTICLE VII.
VOTING.

Each representative present at a meeting of the National Convention shall be entitled to one vote. Members entitled to representation, by virtue of past office, shall be entitled to *but* one vote. The ayes and noes may be required and entered upon record at the call of any three members representing different Departments.

ARTICLE VIII.
DISBURSEMENTS.

Disbursements from the National Treasury shall only be in behalf of the objects of the Woman's Relief Corps, or its incidental expenses, and shall be made either by direction of the National Convention or National Council or the Executive Board of the same. All orders for money must be drawn on the National Treasurer by the National Secretary and approved by the National President.

ARTICLE IX.
PROVISIONAL OFFICERS.

SECTION 1. When three Corps have been formed where no Department organization exists, the National President may appoint a Provisional President who shall assume command, and with the approval of the National President, appoint a Senior and Junior Vice-President, Secretary, Treasurer, and Chaplain ; these officers, with the Provisional President, shall constitute the Provisional Council, and for the time being have all the powers and duties of permanent Department Officers; and when the complement of five Corps has been formed, may proceed with a call for convention and the organization of a permanent Department, by and with the advice of the National President.

SECTION 2. The terms of Provisional Officers expire with the appointing power, they however hold office until their successors are installed.

CHAPTER V.

GENERAL RULES.

ARTICLE I.

REPORTS.

SECTION 1. Each Corps Secretary shall forward through the Corps President quarterly reports to the Department Secretary on the first days of January, April, July and October; she shall at the same time forward the names of rejected applicants, not previously reported. The name of a person dishonorably discharged shall be forwarded to Headquarters without delay. See Chap. V, Art. VII, Sec. 3.

SECTION 2. Each Department Secretary shall, upon receipt of reports, note thereon the date of reception, and turn over the Corps Treasurers' reports to the Department Treasurer. She shall consolidate the quarterly reports of Corps Secretaries on Form C, for the information of the Department President, within twenty days after the beginning of each quarter and prepare a copy of the same to be forwarded by the Department President to the National Secretary, on or before the twentieth day of each quarter. She shall prepare a duplicate copy of Election Returns on Form M to be forwarded to the Secretary of the National W. R. C. Home Board. She shall also make such supplemental reports as may be required by National Headquarters. Corps failing to report in time for the consolidation shall be marked suspended, for that quarter, and their membership shall not be counted in returns.

SECTION 3. The National Secretary shall, upon receipt of reports, note thereon the date of reception, and turn over the Department Treasurer's reports to the National Treasurer. She shall consolidate the reports of the Department Secretaries, for the information of the National President, and present an annual report to the National Convention.

SECTION 4. Each Corps Treasurer shall make a quarterly report on Form B to the Department Treasurer, to be forwarded by the Corps President to the Department Secretary on the first days of January, April, July and October.

SECTION 5. Each Department Treasurer shall consolidate the Corps Treasurers' reports on Form D, for the information of the Department President, within twenty days after the beginning of each quarter, and prepare a copy to be forwarded by the Department President to the National Secretary on or before the twentieth day of each quarter. She shall also make such supplemental reports as may be required by National Headquarters.

SECTION 6. The National Treasurer shall consolidate the Department Treasurers' reports, and prepare and forward a copy to the National President for her information, and present an annual report to National Convention. She shall also make such supplemental reports as may be required by National Headquarters.

ARTICLE II.

ELECTION RETURNS.

SECTION 1.   Corps Installing Officers shall, immediately after installation, forward to the Department Secretary, on Corps Election Return olanks, Form L, certified to as correct by the retiring President, a list of newly elected Corps officers, delegates and alternates to Department Convention, the names of all Past Corps Presidents belonging to the Corps and entitled to seats in Department Convention, also the names of all members in good standing who have held the position of Department President, National President or National Senior or Junior Vice-Presidents, National Secretary or National Treasurer, Department Secretary or Department Treasurer, and shall forward a copy of the same to the Department Instituting and Installing Officer.

SECTION 2.   Department Installing officers shall, immediately after installation, forward to the National Secretary, on Department Election Return blanks, Form M, certified to as correct by the retiring President, a list of newly elected Department officers, delegates and alternates to National Convention, the names of all Past Department Presidents entitled to seats in National Convention; also the names of all members in good standing who have held the position of National President, National Senior or Junior Vice-Presidents, National Secretary or National Treasurer, and shall forward a copy of the same to the National Instituting and Installing Officer.

ARTICLE III.

DUES.

SECTION 1.   Each Corps, either through its By-Laws or by a vote at the last meeting in December, shall assess upon its members a sum payable quarterly on the first days of January, April, July and October, to be known as quarterly dues.   These dues include the per capita tax due the Department.   Members pay dues for the quarter in which they are initiated.

SECTION 2.   Each Department Convention, at its annual session, shall assess a per capita tax on each Corps in its jurisdiction, not exceeding one dollar per annum on each member therein.   This tax shall be drawn from the general fund of the Corps, the amount to be determined by the number of members in good standing as reported by the Corps President on the first days of January, April, July, and October, and shall be forwarded in quarterly instalments by the Corps President to the Department Secretary, payable to the Department Treasurer, who shall receipt therefor.   Corps pay per capita tax for the quarter in which they are organized.

SECTION 3.   The National Convention, at its annual session, shall assess a per capita tax on each Department not exceeding twenty-four cents per annum on each and every member in good standing therein, payable in quarterly instalments, to be forwarded by the Department President to the National Secretary, payable to the order of National Treasurer (who shall receipt therefor), on or before the twentieth day of January, April, July and October.   The amount of quarterly tax due from each Department shall be determined by the number of members in good standing therein, on the first day of the current quarter, as reported by the Department President.

ARTICLE IV.

ARREARAGES.

SECTION 1. Any member of a Corps who is six months in arrears for dues shall be prohibited from voting, shall be ineligible to any office in the Woman's Relief Corps, and shall be reported "suspended" in the quarterly reports to Department Headquarters, until such dues are paid. While so reported, the Corps shall not be subject to the per capita tax on such member, and she shall not be counted in the representation of the Corps in the Department Convention, nor of the Department in the National Convention; provided, however, that when a member is unable by reason of sickness or misfortune to pay her dues, they may be remitted by a two-thirds vote of the members voting at a regular meeting of the Corps. The amount of dues thus remitted shall be paid directly to the member and she shall pay it to the Treasurer in the regular order, that both transactions may be carried on the Treasurer's books.

SECTION 2. If a member be one year in arrears for dues, she shall be dropped from the roll, and reinstated only (on regular application) by the Corps which dropped her, on a two-thirds vote by ballot of all members present and voting at a regular meeting, and upon payment of a sum to be determined by a two-thirds vote of members present and voting at a regular meeting; said sum not to be less than the amount charged as initiation fee. If elected, she shall be re-obligated by the Corps from which she was dropped, or upon the written request of the Corps reinstating her, she may be re-obligated in any Corps within whose jurisdiction she may reside.

SECTION 3. Any Corps in arrears for reports or dues shall be excluded from all representation in the Department Convention until the same are forwarded.

SECTION 4. Any Department in arrears for reports or dues shall be excluded from all representation in the National Convention until the same are forwarded.

ARTICLE V.

INSPECTION.

SECTION 1. There shall be a thorough inspection of each Corps every year, during the months of September, October and November, excepting in such Departments as shall by a two-thirds vote at an annual meeting decide upon other three consecutive months, by the Department Inspector, Assistant Inspectors, or other members assigned to such duty, a report of the same to be forwarded to the Department Inspector immediately thereafter. Such additional inspection shall be made as the Department President may deem necessary, on the recommendation of the Department Inspector, or when directed by the National Inspector. The Department Inspector shall forward Assistant Inspector's Blanks Form O to Assistant Inspectors, and consolidate the same on consolidated report of Department Inspector Form F, for the information of the Department President, and prepare a copy to be forwarded through the Department President to the National Inspector not later than June 1. She shall prepare a summary of inspection and send with her consolidated report to National Inspector.

SECTION 2. Each Department President shall divide her Department into such number of inspection Districts as she deems necessary, changing the same at her discretion.

She shall, on the nomination of the Department Inspector, appoint Assistant Inspectors, who shall be assigned to duty and serve during the pleasure of the Department President.

SECTION 3. Assistant National Inspectors shall be appointed by the National President on the nomination of the National Inspector, and on resigning their position shall forward their resignation direct to the National Inspector. They shall inspect the work and examine the Books and Records of Department officers, under direction of National Inspector, within three days prior to Department Convention, shall report the result of the same immediately, and perform such other duties as may be required of them by the National President or National Inspector.

SECTION 4. The National Inspector shall prescribe the form of blanks to be used for the inspection of Corps, and with the approval of the National President may give such special instructions in reference to inspections as may be deemed necessary. She shall forward Assistant Inspector's blanks Form O, to Inspectors of Detached Corps, Department Inspector's blanks, Form P, to Department Inspectors, and Assistant National Inspector's blanks Form R, to Assistant National Inspectors. She shall consolidate reports of Assistant National Inspectors on Form S, and Department Inspectors on Form T, for the information of the National President, and present a report to the National Convention.

SECTION 5. All books, papers, accounts, records and proceedings pertaining to the Woman's Relief Corps, shall be subject to inspection at all times by the several inspecting officers in their respective districts.

ARTICLE VI.
APPEALS.

All members have the right of appeal to the next higher authority, through the proper channels, from acts of Corps Presidents or Corps, and Department Presidents or Department Conventions to the National President, whose decision shall be final, unless reversed by the National Convention; but all decisions appealed from shall have full force and effect until reversed by proper authority. Appeals must be taken within sixty days from date of rendering official decision. Appeals carried to and acted upon by a National Convention are beyond the jurisdiction of and cannot be reviewed by a National President, unless by vote of Convention they be referred to the incoming National President.

ARTICLE VII.
DISCIPLINE.

SECTION 1. Offences cognizable by the Woman's Relief Corps shall be:

1. Disloyalty to the United States, or violation of the pledge to perpetuate the objects of this association.
2. Disobedience of Rules and Regulations or of lawful orders.
3. Conduct prejudicial to good order and discipline.

SECTION 2. Penalties to either are:
1. Dishonorable discharge.
2. Suspension for a specified period.
3. Reprimand, at the discretion of the Court.

SECTION 3. A member can be dishonorably discharged only upon due trial and sentence as provided in this Article.

SECTION 4. All accusations against any member of the Woman's Relief Corps shall be made in form of written charges and specifications and shall be read before the Corps at a regular meeting, notice of such charges being entertained having been given at the last meeting of the Corps. Charges must be sustained by a majority vote of the Corps, and expenses of the court of inquiry borne by the Corps.

SECTION 5. Charges having been preferred against an officer, she may be suspended from the duties of her office by Corps, Department or National Presidents in their respective jurisdictions.

SECTION 6. Corps, Department and National Presidents, in their respective jurisdictions, shall have discretionary power, after having investigated said charges and specifications, to convene a Court of Inquiry for the examination of alleged offences. Provided, however, that in cases where a Corps President decides it unnecessary to convene such Court, an appeal may be taken by the Corps.

SECTION 7. A Court of Inquiry shall consist of not less than five unprejudiced members in good standing in the Order. An officer shall be tried by a court of her peers.

SECTION 8. Where Department cases demand National investigation, the expense must be borne by the Department.

SECTION 9. The accused shall be given notice at least ten days before the trial takes place. Said notice shall contain a copy of the charges and specifications, and shall name the time and place of trial. If personal service of said notice cannot be had, depositing it in U. S. Mail, addressed to the last known Post Office address of the accused, shall be considered due notice.

SECTION 10. Any member of the Order in good standing may be summoned to give testimony at a Court of Inquiry on her honor as a woman. Only members of the Woman's Relief Corps are allowed to participate in a Court of Inquiry, except when called as witnesses.

SECTION 11. The evidence being concluded, a vote shall be taken on each charge and specification as to the guilt or innocence of the accused, a majority vote being necessary to a decision. The grade of punishment shall be: 1st, Dishonorable Discharge; 2nd, Suspension; 3rd, Reprimand. Should the accused be found guilty, the Court shall proceed to vote upon the grade of punishment, commencing with the highest. Should a majority vote in the negative, they shall proceed to vote upon the next in like manner until a grade of punishment is arrived at.

SECTION 12. The sentence of a Court of Inquiry shall not be carried into effect until the proceedings have been submitted to the officer by whose order the Court was convened, for confirmation or disapproval, and orders in the case. And no sentence of dishonorable discharge shall be carried into effect until the sentence has been approved by the officer next superior to the one ordering the Court.

SECTION 13. The findings or sentence of Courts of Inquiry shall be promulgated through special orders for the Department in which the trouble originated, sending such orders outside of this Department to members of the National Staff and Departments only.

SECTION 14. Department and National Presidents, as reviewing Officers in Court of Inquiry proceedings, may, with the advice and consent of their Council, revise, remit or reduce the sentence of a Court of Inquiry in meritorious cases, according to their best judgment.

SECTION 15. All papers which have been forwarded to National Headquarters for investigation are the property of the Order and must be filed at National Headquarters until disposed of by National Convention.

ARTICLE VIII.

SECRECY.

SECTION 1. *The Ritual and unwritten work of the Woman's Relief Corps, the names of persons causing the rejection of applicants for membership, or any information as to the cause or means of such rejection shall be kept secret;* but any part of proceedings of Corps may be published if ordered by vote of Corps, and any part of the proceedings of a Department Convention may be published if ordered by the Department Convention or Department Council, and any part of the proceedings of the National Convention may be published if ordered by the National Convention or National Council.

SECTION 2. *All discussions of matters secret to the Order in presence of persons not members of the Woman's Relief Corps shall be a violation of the obligation of secrecy.*

SECTION 3. *A member convicted of divulging any of the secrets of the Woman's Relief Corps, or of violating any of the provisions of this Article, may be dishonorably discharged.*

ARTICLE IX.

BONDS.

SECTION 1. Corps Treasurers are required to give bonds in a sum to be named by the Corps, with sufficient sureties, for the faithful discharge of their duties. The bond to be given, and accepted by the Corps *before* installation.

SECTION 2. Department Treasurers shall give bonds in a sum to be named by the Department Convention, with sufficient sureties for the faithful discharge of their duties.

SECTION 3. The National Treasurer shall give bonds in the sum of five thousand dollars, or such amount as shall be voted by National Convention, with sufficient sureties for the faithful discharge of her duties.

SECTION 4. The National Secretary shall give bonds in the sum of one thousand dollars, or such amount as shall be voted by National Convention, with sufficient sureties ior the faithful discharge of her duties.

SECTION 5. The bonds of the above-named officers shall be approved and held by their respective Presidents as trustees.

ARTICLE X.
RELIEF FUND.

A relief fund shall be established by the several Corps, for the assistance of needy Union soldiers, sailors and marines, and their families, and widows and orphans of deceased Union soldiers, sailors and marines. Any donations to this fund shall be held sacred for such purpose.

A relief fund shall be established by each Department Convention, to be disbursed by order of the Department President, through the regular channels. A relief fund shall be established by the National Convention, to be similarly dispensed. Department and National funds may be applied to cases not covered by subordinate Corps.

ARTICLE XI.
MEMORIAL DAY.

The National Convention hereby ordains the observance of Memorial Day, on the 30th of May, enjoining its members to aid and assist the Grand Army of the Republic in commemorating the deeds of their fallen comrades, and that they do all in their power to bring about a proper recognition of the day and its sacred customs.

ARTICLE XII.
PROXIES.

No proxy or substitute can act or be installed in place of a regular representative, either in Corps, Department or National deliberative bodies of the Woman's Relief Corps.

ARTICLE XIII.
TITLES OF ADDRESS.

In the meetings of the several bodies of the Woman's Relief Corps, officers shall be addressed by the title of their office.

ARTICLE XIV.
PAST OFFICERS.

Past officers withdrawing from the Order lose all honors they may have gained. To regain these honors they must be earned by actual service.

ARTICLE XV.
ENGROSSING CHARTERS.

Department and Detached Corps Charters must be engrossed at National Headquarters.

ARTICLE XVI.

DISPOSITION OF CORRESPONDENCE.

All old official correspondence, not needed for future reference, may be destroyed.

ARTICLE XVII.

CONTRIBUTIONS FOR MEMORIAL DAY.

All contributions from Corps and Departments for Memorial Halls and Memorial Day in the South shall be sent through the regular channels to the National Treasurer, who shall forward the same to the Quartermaster-General of the Grand Army of the Republic for distribution among the most worthy and needy Posts.

ARTICLE XVIII.

REVISIONS.

All revisions authorized by the National Convention shall be made by the retiring National President and Secretary, not later than sixty days after National Convention.

ARTICLE XIX.

BADGES.

SECTION 1. The membership badge of the Woman's Relief Corps shall be, in form and material, that adopted at National Convention held in Minneapolis, July 23d, 1884, and no other shall be worn as the badge of the Woman's Relief Corps, except that prescribed for Officers and Past Officers, and must be obtained from National Headquarters through the proper channels.

This badge is a Maltese cross of copper bronze, with the Grand Army medallion suspended from a bar pin, bearing the initials "F. C. L." (Fraternity, Charity, Loyalty), by a red, white and blue ribbon, one and one-half inches long in the clear, and one and one-fourth inches in width.

SECTION 2. The official badge is the same, except that the bar pin designates the office, and the ribbon is of solid color, blue designating the Corps, red the Department, and yellow the National.

This badge may be worn by all Corps, Department or National officers in the Woman's Relief Corps, when on duty or on occasions of ceremony.

SECTION 3. Assistant Inspectors, Assistant Instituting and Installing Officers, Department or National, shall wear a white ribbon one-half inch wide over the ribbon of their badges, lengthwise in the centre.

SECTION 4. The Memorial Badge is a neat bow of black gros grain ribbon, one inch wide, fastened just above the badge so as to partly conceal it.

SECTION 5. The Recognition Pin is a small Maltese cross of copper bronze, bearing the initials "W. R. C." and "1883" (the year of National organization) on its points. Has raised centre-piece, with "F. C. L." on diagonal bar. Is also made in gold, with centre in tri-colored enamel. The pin is designed as a means of recognition among members.

SECTION 6. Past officers are entitled to wear the past rank badge of the highest position they have held in the Woman's Relief Corps.

Past rank is designated as follows: To the bar pin of Past Corps officers is suspended a copper bronze shield. To the bar pin of Past Department officers a silver shield. To the bar pin of Past National elected officers, also Past National Secretaries, Treasurers, Inspectors, Counselors and Instituting and Installing Officers a red Geneva Cross. To the bar pin of all other Past National *appointed* officers a gilt or gold shield.

SECTION 7. No member shall be allowed to sit in Corps meeting or Convention without wearing the badge, unless excused by vote in special cases.

SECTION 8. Corps officers badges are Corps property, belong to the Corps, and revert with office.

Badges of all Department and National Officers, both elected and appointed, belong to and revert with office.

Retired officers desiring past rank badges, must procure them through their Corps or Department Presidents.

SECTION 9. Officers of new Corps having paid for, but not received a membership badge, shall upon retiring from office, receive from the Corps a past rank badge.

SECTION 10. Before receiving an honorable discharge from the Order, members must return their badge to the Corps of which they are a member and are entitled to receive the regular price therefor.

SECTION 11. Officers of disbanded Corps are entitled to past officers' badges, provided they join another Corps in the same Department before the expiration of their transfer card.

ARTICLE XX.
LETTERS DESIGNATING FREE BLANKS.

*A. — Corps Secretary.
*B. — Corps Treasurer.
C. — Department Secretary.
D. — Department Treasurer.
E. — Department Secretary's Consolidated Blank.
F. — Department Treasurer's Consolidated Blank.
*G. — Assistant Instituting and Installing Officer. (Corps.)
H. — Department Instituting and Installing Officer. (Dept.)
I. — National Instituting and Installing Officer. (Consolidated.)
*J. — Corps Chaplain, "Memorial Day Blank."
K. — Department Chaplain, National Chaplain.
*L. — Corps Election Returns. — (Corps Installing Officer's Report.)
M. — Dept. Election Returns. — (Dept. Installing Officer's Report.)
*N. — Corps Relief.
*O. — Assistant Inspector.
P. — Department Inspector.
R. — Assistant National Inspector.
S. — Consolidated Report of Assistant National Inspector.
T. — Consolidated Report of Department Inspector.
*U. — Consolidated Report of Corps Installation.
V. — Department Delinquent Reports.

☞ NOTE.— For distribution of Free Blanks see third page of cover.
* Blanks marked (*), also Charter Application Blanks and Department Requisition Books, must be ordered by Department Treasurer from National Treasurer on regular requisition blanks.

ARTICLE XXI.

OFFICIAL COMMUNICATIONS.

Communications are to be made on letter paper, folded in three equal parts, and endorsed on the first fold in the following manner:

HEADQUARTERS . . . . CORPS, No. . . . . .)
DEPARTMENT OF . . . . W. R. C., }
AUXILIARY TO THE G. A. R.)

———,   — - ·   ———, 18 . .

A . . . . B . . . .

President.

[Here give brief statement of contents.]

Reply will be made by endorsement through the different channels required. Members address Corps Secretaries; Corps Presidents the Department Secretary; Department Presidents the National Secretary. From National Headquarters to Corps the reverse rule is followed. The National Secretary addresses the Department President, and the Department Secretary the Corps President.

As a matter of convenience the Department Secretary may address the National Secretary on subjects of routine business.

FORMS.

[FOR A MEMBER IN THE CORPS.]

———————————————————, 18 . . .

A . . . . . . D . . . . . . ,
        Secretary . . . . . . Corps, No. . . . .

Madam:

       I respectfully ask a decision on the following point:

* * * * * * * * * * * * * * * * * * * * * * * * *

Yours in F. C. and L.,

       L . . . . . . L . . . . .

[CORPS TO DEPARTMENT.]

HEADQUARTERS . . CORPS, No. . . . DEPARTMENT . . W. R. C.)
AUXILIARY TO THE G. A. R. {

——— -   — - ————————, 18 . .

———————————— . . . —— .. ——.,

       Secretary Department of . . . . .

Madam:

* * * * * * * * * * * * * * * * * * * * * * *

Yours in F. C. and L.,

       G . . . . H . . . . .

Corps President.

[DEPARTMENT TO NATIONAL HEADQUARTERS.]

HEADQUARTERS DEPARTMENT OF . . . . . . W. R. C., }
           AUXILIARY TO THE G. A. R. }

I . . . . . J . . . . . ,

        National Secretary, W. R. C.

Madam :

  *   *   *   *   *   *   *   *   *   *   *   *   *

Yours in F., C. and L.,

K . . . . . L . . . . .

Department President.

ORDERS.

Orders received by Corps must be read in regular order of business, at the next meeting after being received. No vote is necessary on their reception. If business is suggested it lays over until "New Business"; otherwise the orders will be duly filed. All official orders issued by Corps and Departments will follow in style and size those issued from National Headquarters.

THE OFFICIAL ORDERS *of a Corps* will be signed:

  *   *   *   *   *   *   *   *   *   *   *   *

By order of A . . . . . B . . . . . , Corps President.

C . . . . . D . . . . . ,

Corps Secretary.

[*Of a Department.*]

By command of E . . . . . F . . . . . , Department President.

G . . . . . H . . . . . ,

Department Secretary.

[*Of National Headquarters.*]

By command of I . . . . . J . . . . . , National President.

K . . . . . L . . . . . ,

National Secretary

RULES OF ORDER

FOR THE NATIONAL CONVENTION.

[*May also be used in so far as they apply in Department Conventions.*]

SECTION 1. ORDER OF BUSINESS.

1. Opening of the National Convention in due form.
2. Calling Roll of Officers.
3. Report of Committee on Credentials, appointed prior to Convention, the National Secretary, Chairman.
4. Calling roll of members.
5. Reports of officers, beginning with that of the National President.
6. Appointment of committees, to consist of five members each, as follows:

    1st. Committee on Resolutions.
    2d. Committee on Reports of Officers.
    3d. Committee on Rules and Regulations and Ritual.

7. Reception and reference of communications from Department Conventions, to be called according to seniority.
8. Reception and reference of communications from individuals.
9. Reports of Committees.
10. Unfinished business.
11. New business.
12. Election and Installation of Officers.
13. At the second and each succeeding session the minutes of the preceding session shall be read immediately after the opening ceremonies. This shall also be done before the closing exercises at the last session.
14. The most important business, including the election of officers, shall be made the special order of business not later than the afternoon of the second day.
15. This order of business may be suspended at any time for a definite purpose, by a two-thirds vote of the National Convention to be taken without debate.

SECTION 2. The National President shall state every question properly presented to the National Convention, and before putting it to vote shall ask, "Is the Convention ready for the question?"

Should no member offer to speak she shall rise to put the question, and after she has risen no further discussion will be in order.

SECTION 3. The National President may speak to points of order in preference to other members, rising for that purpose. She shall announce all votes and decisions, and decide questions of order, subject to an appeal to the National Convention, by any two members, which appeal, if required, shall be in writing.

SECTION 4. When an appeal is taken from the decision of the presiding officer, said officer shall surrender the chair to the officer next in rank, who shall put the question thus: "Shall the decision of the chair stand as the judgment of the National Convention?"

SECTION 5. When the decision of any vote is doubted, the National President shall direct the National Secretary to count the vote in the affirmative and negative, and report the result to her.

SECTION 6. When two or more members rise to speak at the same time, the National President will decide who is entitled to the floor.

SECTION 7. A motion must be seconded and stated by the National President before any action thereon is in order and if required by any two members, shall be reduced to writing.

SECTION 8. A motion may be withdrawn by the mover and seconder before a vote is had thereon, and, if withdrawn, no record thereof shall be made on the minutes.

SECTION 9. The name of a member making a motion or offering any business shall be entered on the minutes.

SECTION 10. A division of a question containing two or more distinct propositions may be demanded by any member.

SECTION 11. Should a member wish to speak she will rise and respectfully address the National President, confining her remarks to the question before the National Convention, and avoid personalities and unbecoming language.

SECTION 12. No member shall be interrupted while speaking, except by a call to order, or by a member to explain.

SECTION 13. No member shall speak more than twice upon the same question, except for explanation when misrepresented, nor longer than ten minutes at any time, without a vote of the National Convention, to be taken without debate.

SECTION 14. No member shall, in debate, impeach the motives of a fellow member, treat her with personal disrespect, or pass between her and the chair while she is speaking.

SECTION 15. Any conversation calculated to disturb a member while speaking, or to hinder the transaction of business, shall be deemed a violation of order, and if persisted in shall incur censure.

SECTION 16. On questions of order there shall be no debate, unless the National President shall invite it, or unless an appeal is taken.

SECTION 17. When a member is called to order, she shall at once take her seat until her point of order is decided.

SECTION 18. When a member is called to order for words spoken in debate, the objectionable words shall, if required, be reduced to writing.

SECTION 19. When a question is before the National Convention, the only motions in order shall be:

1. To adjourn.
2. To lay on the table.
3. The previous question.
4. To postpone indefinitely.
5. To postpone to a definite period.
6. To postpone.
7. To refer.
8. To amend.

To take precedence in the order named, and the first three to be decided without debate.

SECTION 20. When the previous question is moved and seconded, it shall preclude all other motions and debate. It shall be put in this form: "Shall the main question be now put?" If decided in the affirmative, the vote shall be at once taken, without debate and in the same order as if the previous question had not been ordered.

SECTION 21. A motion to adjourn shall always be in order, except:

1. While a member is speaking.
2. While a vote is being taken.
3. When to adjourn was the last preceding motion.

A motion to adjourn cannot be amended, but when to adjourn to a given time or place, it is open to amendment or debate.

SECTION 22. The reading of any paper relating to the subject under consideration shall always be in order.

SECTION 23. When a blank is to be filled, the question shall be first taken on the highest sum or number, or longest time, or in the order of nomination, if it is to be filled with the name of a person.

SECTION 24. The yeas and nays may be required and entered upon the minutes at the call of any three members representing different Departments, as provided in Chap. IV, Article VII, Rules and Regulations.

SECTION 25. When a matter is postponed indefinitely it shall not again be in order at the same session of the National Convention.

SECTION 26. But two amendments can be pending at the same time.

SECTION 27. A motion to reconsider shall be in order at any time during the same session of the National Convention, but must be made by those voting with the majority, or those voting in the negative in the case of equal division. A motion to reconsider once made and negatived shall not be renewed at the same session.

SECTION 28. All reports and resolutions must be submitted in writing, and when from a committee they must be signed by a majority of such committee.

SECTION 29. All members entitled to vote shall vote on all questions, unless excused by a vote of the National Convention, to be taken without debate.

SECTION 30. When a majority report is followed by a report from the minority of a committee, the former, after being read, shall lie upon the table until the latter is presented, after which, upon motion, either may be considered.

SECTION 31. When a report has been read it shall be considered properly before the National Convention, without any motion to accept.

SECTION 32. When a report is submitted with a resolution attached, action shall be had on the resolution only, unless the report be considered improper or incomplete, when it shall be recommitted. When no resolution accompanies the report, such report may be altered or amended.

SECTION 33. No report or resolution properly before the National Convention shall be withdrawn without its permission, to be given or refused without debate.

SECTION 34. Questions not debatable.

1. To adjourn, when to adjourn simply.
2. To lay on the table.
3. For the previous question.
4. To take up any particular item of business.
5. Granting leave to speak.
6. Granting leave to withdraw a report or resolution.
7. To excuse from voting.
8. Questions of order, where no appeal has been taken, or where the National President has been invited to discuss.

SECTION 35. These Rules of Order may be altered or amended at any regular session of the National Convention, upon proposition in writing, and by a two-thirds vote of those present and voting.

INDEX TO RULES AND REGULATIONS.

— --

HEADQUARTERS WOMAN'S RELIEF CORPS,
CHICAGO, ILL., December, 1894.

I certify that the above and foregoing is a true and correct copy of the Rules and Regulations and Rules of Order of the National Convention, Woman's Relief Corps, Auxiliary to the Grand Army of the Republic.

Jennie Bross.

National Secretary.